HEROES IN THE CLASSROOM

rtc
Publishing

Writers of the Round Table Press
PO Box 511
Highland Park, IL 60035

Illustration	NATHAN LUETH
Publisher	COREY MICHAEL BLAKE
Post Production	SUNNY DIMARTINO
Director of Operations	KRISTIN WESTBERG
Facts Keeper	MIKE WINICOUR
Cover Design	NATHAN LUETH, SUNNY DIMARTINO
Interior Design and Layout	SUNNY DIMARTINO
Last Looks	SUNNY DIMARTINO

Printed in the United States of America
First Edition: August 2014
10 9 8 7 6 5 4 3 2 1

Library of Congress Cataloging-in-Publication Data
Westberg, Kristin
Heroes in the classroom: an activity book about bullying / Kristin Westberg with
Jeff Krukar, Pamela DeLoatch, and James G. Balestrieri.—1st ed. p. cm.
Print ISBN: 978-1-939418-63-0
Library of Congress Control Number: 2014945720

RTC Publishing is an imprint of Writers of the Round Table, Inc.
Writers of the Round Table Press and the RTC Publishing logo
are trademarks of Writers of the Round Table, Inc.

HEROES IN THE CLASSROOM

AN ACTIVITY BOOK ABOUT BULLYING

THE ORP LIBRARY

ILLUSTRATED BY
NATHAN LUETH

WRITTEN BY
KRISTIN WESTBERG

WITH
JEFF KRUKAR, PH.D. · PAMELA DeLOATCH · JAMES G. BALESTRIERI

WHAT IS BULLYING?

IN WHICH OF THESE PICTURES DO YOU THINK SOMEONE IS BEING BULLIED?

BULLYING CHECKLIST

HOW DO YOU KNOW IF WHAT YOU'VE SEEN OR
EXPERIENCED IS CONSIDERED BULLYING?
IF ALL FOUR BOXES ARE CHECKED
AS TRUE, IT IS.

☐ THE BEHAVIOR HAS HAPPENED OVER AND OVER AGAIN

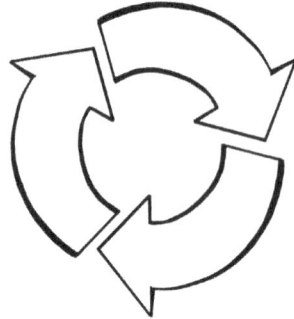

☐ THE SAME PEOPLE ARE INVOLVED EVERY TIME

☐ THE BEHAVIOR WAS CAUSED ON PURPOSE

☐ IT HURT BODY OR FEELINGS

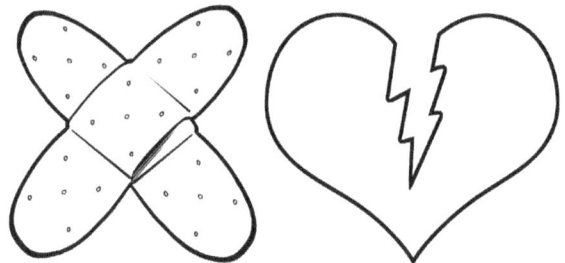

WHAT MIGHT BULLYING LOOK LIKE?

CIRCLE THE WORDS THAT MIGHT BE BULLYING BEHAVIORS

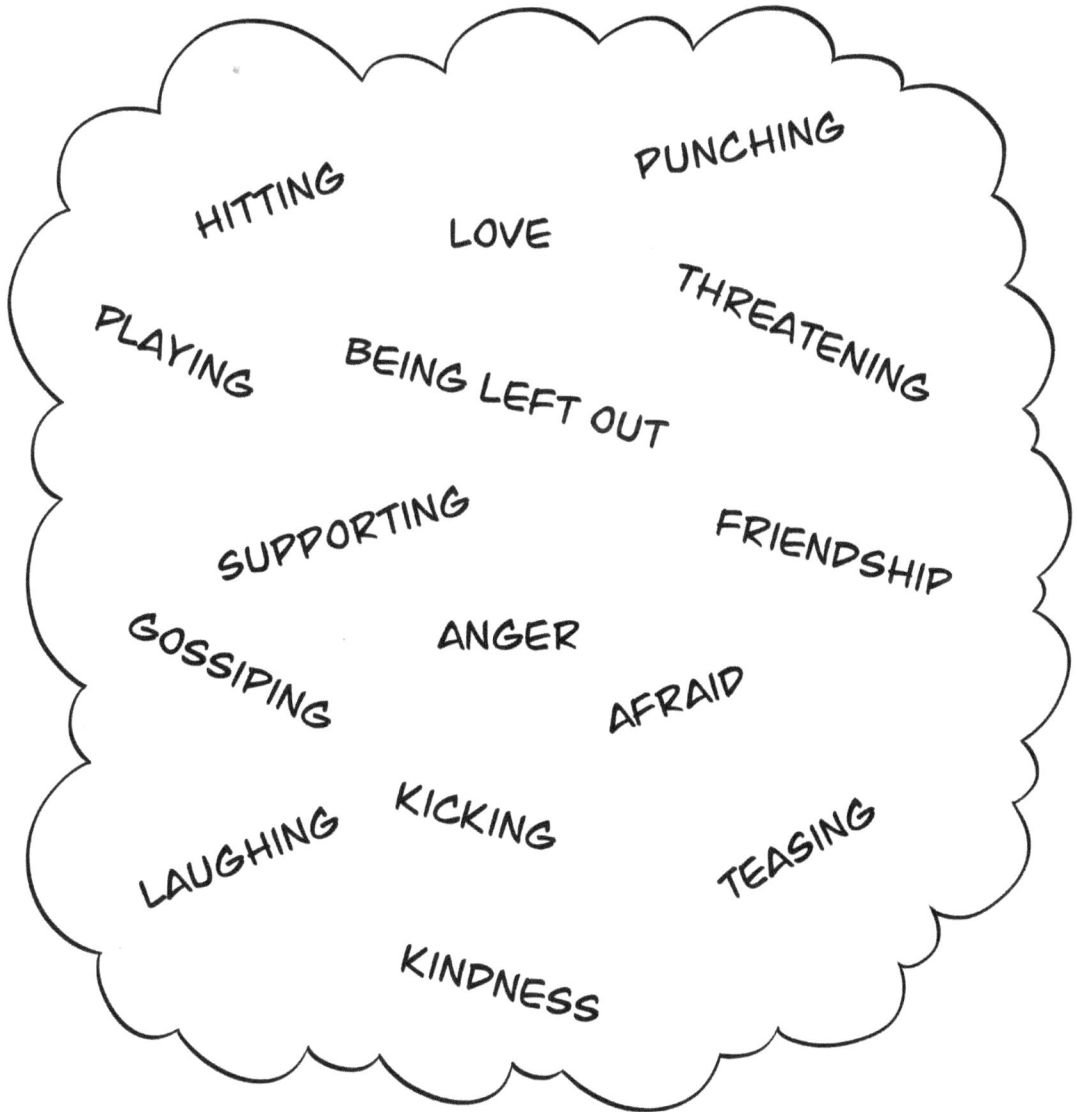

HITTING

PUNCHING

LOVE

THREATENING

PLAYING

BEING LEFT OUT

SUPPORTING

FRIENDSHIP

ANGER

GOSSIPING

AFRAID

KICKING

LAUGHING

TEASING

KINDNESS

DID YOU KNOW?

1 IN 7 STUDENTS IN GRADES K-5 IS EITHER A BULLY OR HAS BEEN BULLIED.

56% OF STUDENTS HAVE SEEN SOME TYPE OF BULLYING AT SCHOOL.

15% OF KIDS MISSING SCHOOL ARE ABSENT BECAUSE THEY'RE AFRAID OF BEING BULLIED.

KIDS WITH DISABILITIES ARE TWO TO THREE TIMES MORE LIKELY TO BE BULLIED THAN KIDS WITHOUT DISABILITIES.

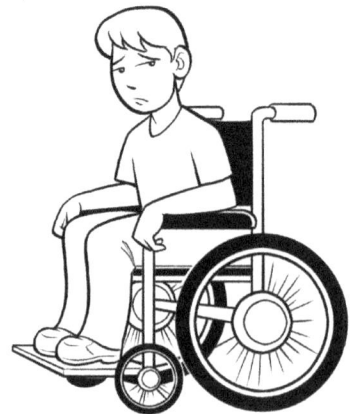

WHAT DOES A BULLY LOOK LIKE?

ANYBODY CAN BE A BULLY.

SOME BULLIES ARE POPULAR AND HAVE LOTS OF FRIENDS.

OTHERS ARE DISLIKED BY ALMOST EVERY-ONE AND SEEM TO NOT HAVE ANY FRIENDS.

BULLIES CANNOT BE RECOGNIZED BY WHAT THEY LOOK LIKE. BULLIES ARE RECOGNIZED BY WHAT THEY SAY OR DO, AND BY THEIR ACTIONS.

ARE YOU A BULLY?

EVEN THE NICEST PERSON CAN BE A BULLY IN CERTAIN SITUATIONS. HAVE YOU EVER DONE ANY OF THE FOLLOWING?

LAUGHED WHEN SOMEONE GETS HURT OR EMBARRASSED

SENT MEAN OR EMBARRASSING TEXT MESSAGES OR EMAILS

MADE SOMEONE DO SOMETHING THEY DIDN'T WANT TO

MADE JOKES ABOUT SOMEONE'S RACE, CULTURE, OR PREFERENCES

STOOD BY AND WATCHED WHILE SOMEONE ELSE WAS BULLIED

IF YOU SAID YES TO ANY OF THESE, YOU MAY HAVE ENGAGED IN BULLYING BEHAVIOR.

WRITE A LETTER

HAVE YOU EVER DONE SOMETHING MEAN TO SOMEONE? WRITING A LETTER IS A GREAT WAY TO APOLOGIZE. USE THE GUIDE BELOW AND TELL THAT PERSON HOW YOU THINK AND FEEL.

DEAR_____,

I WANTED TO WRITE YOU A LETTER TO TELL YOU THAT I AM SORRY FOR

_____

AT THE TIME, THE REASON I DID IT WAS

_____

WHEN IT HAPPENED, I FELT

_____

I UNDERSTAND NOW THAT IT MADE YOU THINK AND FEEL

_____

NEXT TIME, I WILL MAKE SURE IT DOES NOT HAPPEN AGAIN BY

_____

ONCE AGAIN, I'M SORRY.

SINCERELY,

_____

THE BULLYING TRIANGLE

THINK OF A TIME WHEN YOU EXPERIENCED OR WITNESSED BULLYING. WHERE WERE YOU ON THE BULLYING TRIANGLE?

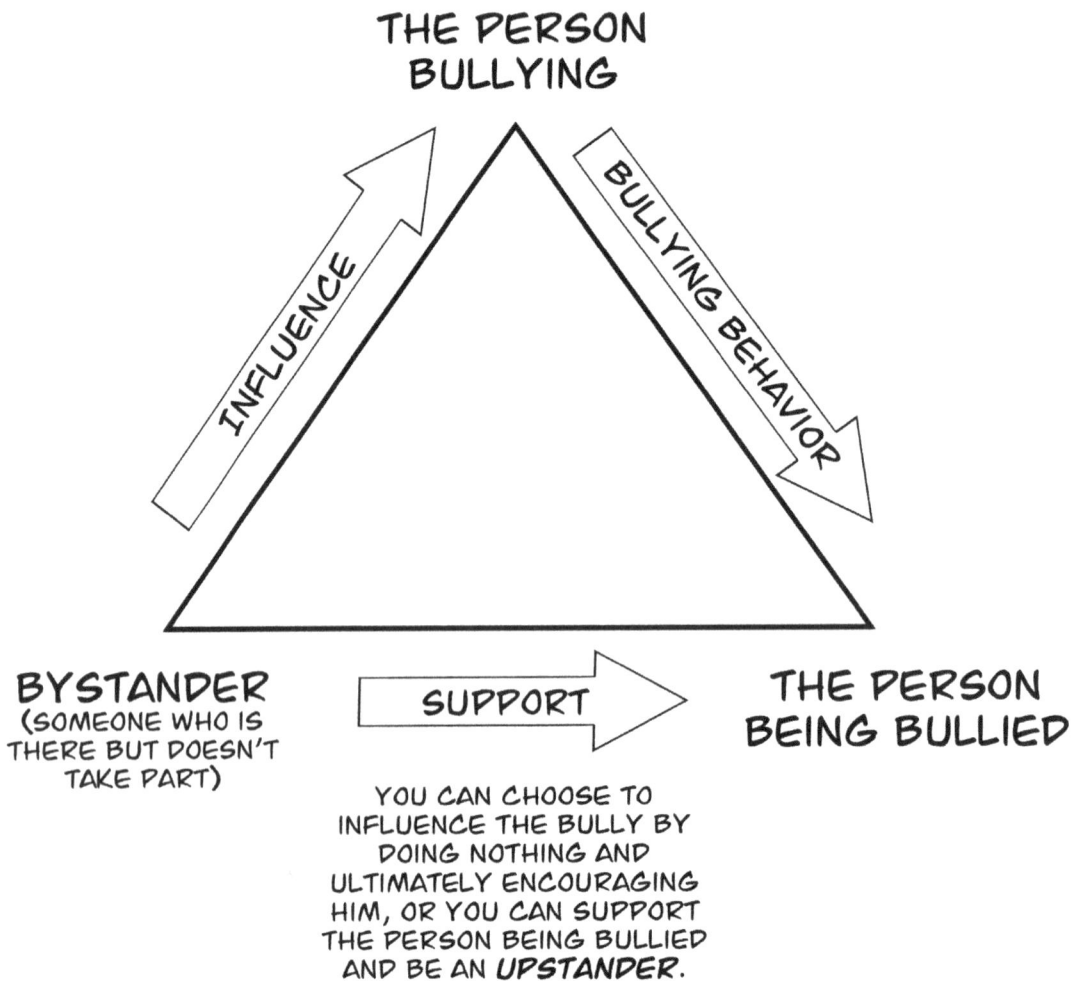

THE PERSON BULLYING

INFLUENCE

BULLYING BEHAVIOR

BYSTANDER
(SOMEONE WHO IS THERE BUT DOESN'T TAKE PART)

SUPPORT

THE PERSON BEING BULLIED

YOU CAN CHOOSE TO INFLUENCE THE BULLY BY DOING NOTHING AND ULTIMATELY ENCOURAGING HIM, OR YOU CAN SUPPORT THE PERSON BEING BULLIED AND BE AN *UPSTANDER*.

EVERYONE PLAYS A ROLE WHEN IT COMES TO BULLYING.

THE EFFECTS OF BULLYING

IN THIS PICTURE, WHO IS DOING THE BULLYING, AND WHO IS BEING BULLIED?

WHEN THE TEACHER IS NOT LOOKING, ALEX FLICKS MATTHEW IN THE EAR AND CALLS HIM A DORK. WHAT WOULD YOU THINK IF THIS HAPPENED TO YOU? HOW WOULD YOU FEEL IF THIS HAPPENED TO YOU?

THE EFFECTS OF BULLYING

IN THIS PICTURE, WHICH PERSON IS DOING THE BULLYING, BEING BULLIED, A BYSTANDER?

SUN-YI HATES GOING TO RECESS BECAUSE THE KIDS REFUSE TO LET HER PLAY WITH THEM. WHAT WOULD YOU THINK IF THIS HAPPENED TO YOU? HOW WOULD YOU FEEL IF THIS HAPPENED TO YOU?

THE EFFECTS OF BULLYING

IN THIS PICTURE, WHO IS DOING THE BULLYING, AND WHO IS BEING BULLIED?

OTHER KIDS KEEP SENDING MICHELLE MEAN TEXT MESSAGES. WHAT WOULD YOU THINK IF THIS HAPPENED TO YOU? HOW WOULD YOU FEEL IF THIS HAPPENED TO YOU?

THE EFFECTS OF BULLYING

IN THIS PICTURE, WHICH PERSON IS DOING THE BULLYING, BEING BULLIED, A BYSTANDER?

ADAM MAKES JOE BUY HIM SNACKS, OR ELSE HE WON'T HANG OUT WITH HIM. WHAT WOULD YOU THINK IF THIS HAPPENED TO YOU? HOW WOULD YOU FEEL IF THIS HAPPENED TO YOU?

THE EFFECTS OF BULLYING

IN THIS PICTURE, WHICH PERSON IS DOING THE BULLYING, BEING BULLIED, A BYSTANDER?

AT RECESS, MARK NEVER LETS TOM PLAY WITH HIS FRIENDS, AND TELLS THEM TO IGNORE HIM. WHAT WOULD YOU THINK IF THIS HAPPENED TO YOU? HOW WOULD YOU FEEL IF THIS HAPPENED TO YOU?

THE EFFECTS OF BULLYING

IN THIS PICTURE, WHICH PERSON IS DOING THE BULLYING, BEING BULLIED, A BYSTANDER?

KELLY IGNORES THE NEW GIRL AND MAKES FUN OF HER HAIR AND CLOTHES BEHIND HER BACK. WHAT WOULD YOU THINK IF THIS HAPPENED TO YOU? HOW WOULD YOU FEEL IF THIS HAPPENED TO YOU?

SO WHY DO PEOPLE BULLY OTHERS?

FIND SOME OF THE REASONS PEOPLE
MIGHT BULLY OTHERS BELOW.

```
A  D  F  G  J  S  S  Z  M  P  X  I
S  C  A  R  E  D  Q  W  E  R  I  M
A  H  N  B  A  T  U  D  U  K  N  M
D  Q  G  X  L  O  N  E  L  Y  S  A
V  C  R  T  O  G  H  M  A  O  E  T
F  F  Y  G  U  L  A  J  S  H  C  U
H  U  R  T  S  D  P  I  H  V  U  R
B  D  R  U  W  C  P  R  A  I  R  E
U  N  S  U  R  E  Y  A  M  F  E  L
O  C  T  F  V  N  Q  Z  E  B  H  Y
M  R  W  O  R  R  I  E  D  K  B  O
```

SCARED	ANGRY	UNHAPPY
HURT	LONELY	SAD
JEALOUS	INSECURE	IMMATURE
UNSURE	WORRIED	ASHAMED

WHAT'S THE BIG DEAL?

COLOR IN SOME OF THE WAYS
SOMEONE WHO IS BULLIED MIGHT FEEL.

CONFUSED

HAPPY

NERVOUS

ANGRY

TIRED

EMBARRASSED

SAD

SCARED

SILLY

SOME OF THE EFFECTS OF BULLYING

CIRCLE THE THINGS BULLYING HAS CAUSED *YOU* TO FEEL OR HAVE HAPPENED TO YOU.

STRESSED

SAD

SCARED

CAN'T THINK WELL

NIGHTMARES

TUMMY ACHES

UNSURE OF MYSELF

DON'T WANT TO EAT

POOR GRADES

WHAT DO BULLYING FEELINGS LOOK LIKE TO YOU?

CUT OUT PICTURES FROM MAGAZINES AND
MAKE A COLLAGE, OR DO YOUR OWN DRAWING
SHOWING HOW PEOPLE WHO ARE BULLIED
MIGHT FEEL.

WHERE CAN BULLYING HAPPEN?

IT CAN HAPPEN ANYWHERE!

- PARK

- CHURCH

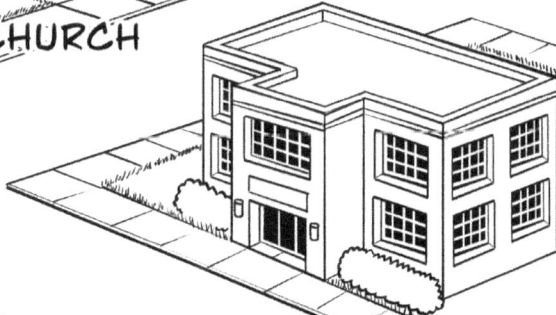

- SCHOOL

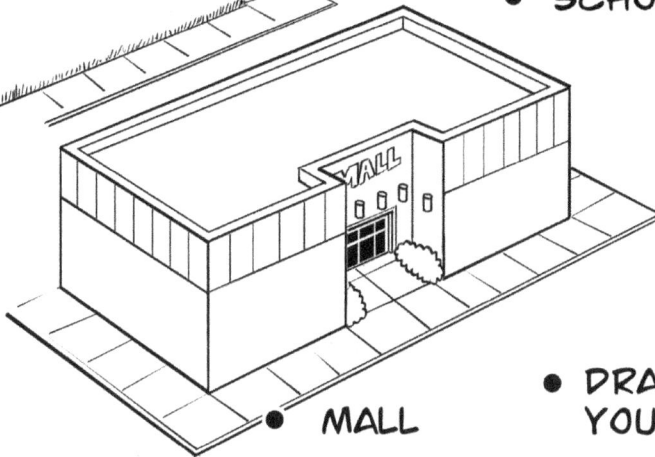

- MALL

- DRAW A PLACE ABOVE WHERE YOU'VE SEEN BULLYING

BULLYING
DOs AND DON'Ts

IF YOU ARE BEING BULLIED, HERE
ARE SOME THINGS YOU CAN DO.

GET AWAY
IF YOU FEEL
UNSAFE.

TELL AN ADULT
OR SOMEONE
YOU TRUST.

AVOID BEING ALONE
WITH THE PERSON
BULLYING YOU.

TELL THE PERSON
BULLYING YOU TO
LEAVE YOU ALONE.

REMEMBER THAT YOU ARE
IMPORTANT. FIND PEOPLE
WHO CARE ABOUT YOU.

BULLYING
DOs AND DON'Ts

IF YOU ARE BEING BULLIED, HERE ARE SOME THINGS NOT TO DO.

DON'T GET PHYSICAL AND TRY TO FIGHT.

TRY NOT TO SHOW FEAR IN FRONT OF THE PERSON BULLYING YOU.

DON'T THREATEN THE PERSON AND CALL THEM NAMES BACK.

DON'T JUST IGNORE THE BULLYING AND HOPE IT STOPS.

DON'T BELIEVE WHAT THE BULLY IS SAYING ABOUT YOU.

BULLYING
DOs AND DON'Ts

IF YOU SEE **OTHERS** BEING BULLIED,
HERE ARE SOME THINGS YOU CAN DO.

SPEAK UP FOR
THE PERSON BEING
BULLIED.

LET THE PERSON
BEING BULLIED KNOW
YOU SUPPORT THEM.

TALK TO AN ADULT
YOU TRUST ABOUT
THE SITUATION.

LET THE BULLY
KNOW THAT WHAT THEY'RE
DOING IS WRONG.

BULLY-PROOF YOURSELF

HERE ARE SOME THINGS TO DO WHEN BULLYING HAPPENS TO YOU.

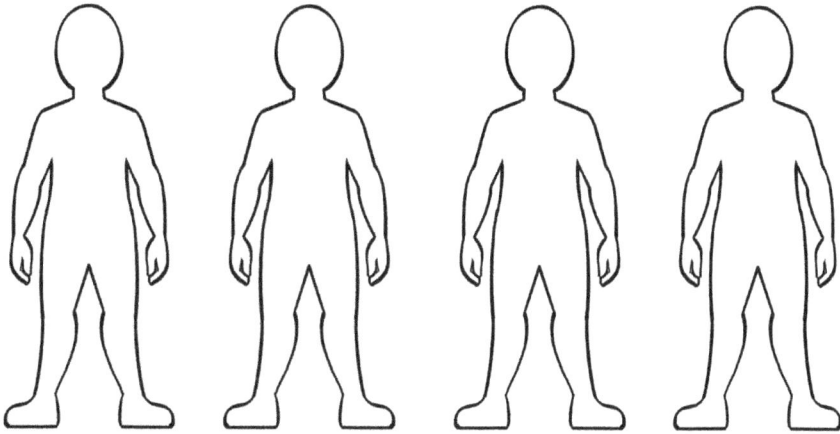

TALK TO AN ADULT. DRAW IN SOME ADULTS YOU KNOW THAT YOU CAN TALK TO IF YOU GET BULLIED. WRITE IN THEIR NAMES, TOO!

DON'T BELIEVE A WORD THEY SAY, NO MATTER WHAT. WHEN A BULLY SAYS SOMETHING THAT ISN'T TRUE, TRY THINKING OF ALL THE GOOD THINGS ABOUT YOURSELF.

BULLY-PROOF YOURSELF

HERE ARE SOME THINGS TO DO WHEN
BULLYING HAPPENS TO YOU.

BE ASSERTIVE. TELL THE BULLY TO LEAVE YOU ALONE WITH A
FIRM VOICE TONE. KNOW WHAT YOU ARE GOING TO SAY WHEN
SOMEONE TRIES TO BULLY YOU.

STAY CALM. OFTEN BULLIES ARE TRYING TO GET A REACTION
OUT OF YOU, SO DON'T GIVE IT TO THEM.

BULLY-PROOF YOURSELF

HERE ARE SOME THINGS TO DO WHEN
BULLYING HAPPENS TO YOU.

EVEN IF YOU DON'T FEEL BRAVE AND STRONG, ACT LIKE IT.

BUILD YOURSELF UP. REMEMBER THAT YOU ARE IMPORTANT,
YOU ARE CARED FOR, AND YOU MATTER!

BULLY-AVOIDANCE

GET THROUGH THE MAZE WITHOUT RUNNING INTO A BULLY. AVOID UNSUPERVISED AREAS WHERE BULLIES STRIKE.

"NO ONE CAN MAKE YOU FEEL INFERIOR WITHOUT YOUR CONSENT."

-ELEANOR ROOSEVELT

WHAT DO YOU THINK ELEANOR ROOSEVELT MEANT WHEN SHE SAID THAT?

MY BULLYING SHIELD

BELIEVING IN YOUR POSITIVE QUALITIES CAN HELP TO
SHIELD YOU FROM THE EFFECTS OF BULLYING. WRITE
POSITIVE WORDS OR REMINDERS ABOUT YOURSELF THAT
HELP PROTECT YOU FROM NEGATIVITY ON THIS SHIELD.

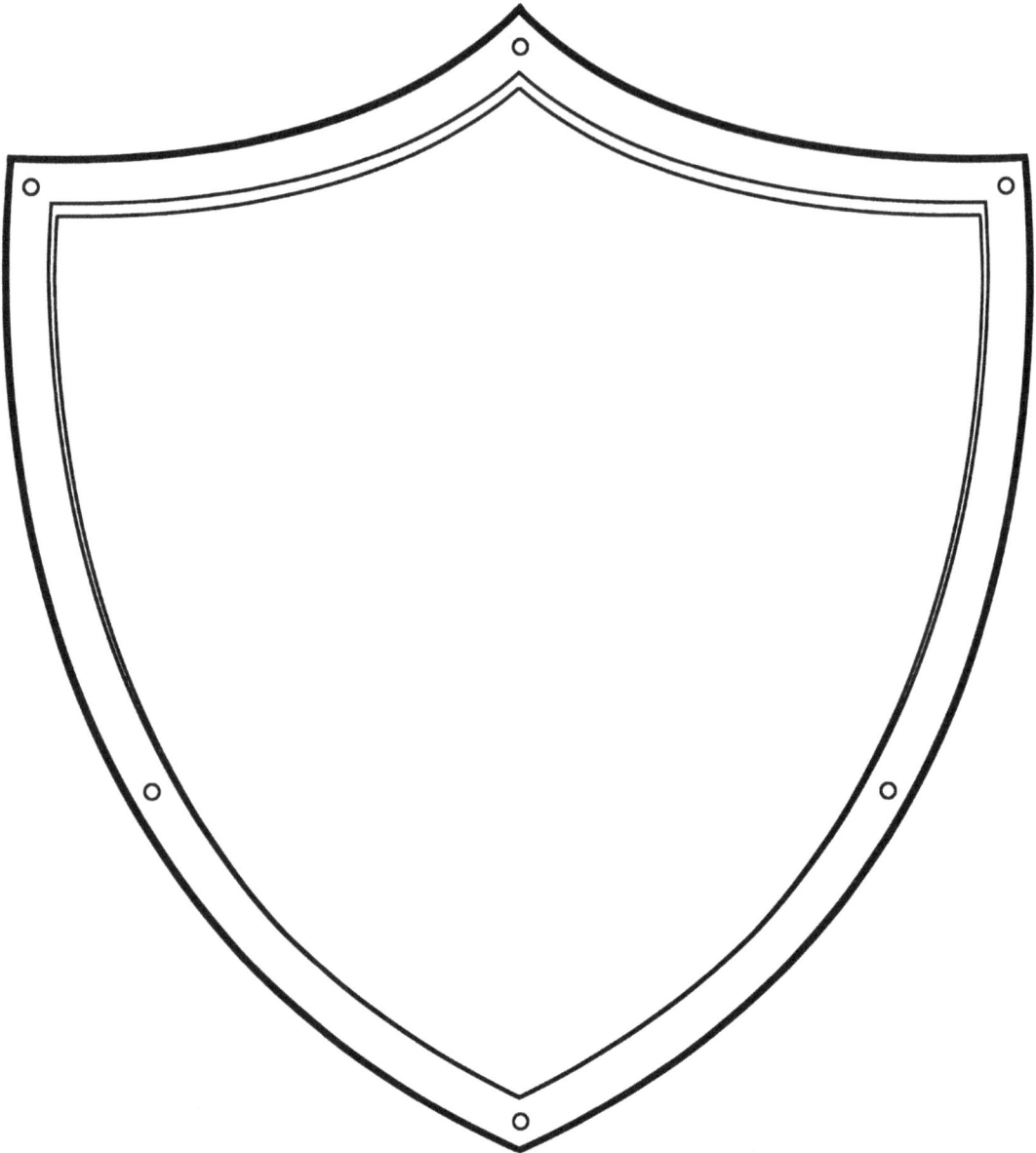

REMEMBER WHO YOU ARE IF YOU'RE BEING BULLIED

CREATE YOUR OWN ANTI-BULLYING "POWER MANTRA" BY FILLING IN THE BLANKS WITH SOMETHING GOOD ABOUT YOURSELF THAT YOU CAN REMEMBER WHEN BEING BULLIED.

I AM   I CAN

_____   _____

I WILL

_____

YOU ARE IMPORTANT!

SOMETIMES YOU NEED TO SEARCH FOR YOUR STRENGTHS. CAN YOU FIND THEM IN THE CROSSWORD BELOW?

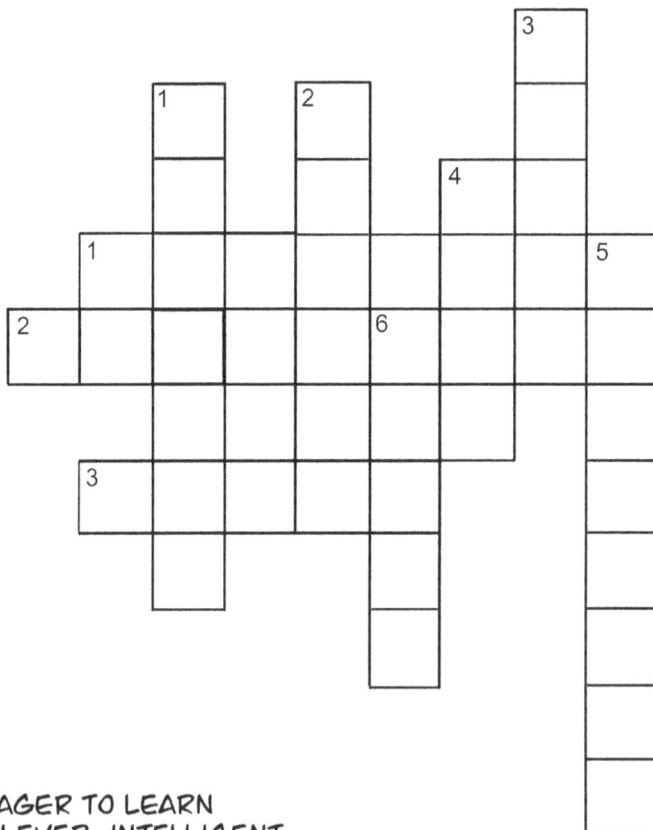

DOWN
1. EAGER TO LEARN
2. CLEVER, INTELLIGENT, 5 LETTERS
3. HAVING COURAGE
4. GOOD-NATURED, CARING
5. UNDERSTANDING ANOTHER'S FEELINGS
6. A TRUE AND _____ FRIEND

ACROSS
1. MAKER OF NEW IDEAS
2. PLAY BY THE RULES, 4 LETTERS
3. INSPIRING LAUGHTER

BRAVE
CREATIVE

SMART
LOYAL

EMPATHIC
FUNNY

CURIOUS
KIND
FAIR

REMEMBER THOSE WHO LOVE, CARE, AND SUPPORT YOU!

WHEN YOU'RE FEELING DOWN, REMEMBER THAT THERE ARE PEOPLE WHO LOVE, CARE, AND SUPPORT YOU NO MATTER WHAT. USE THE SPACE BELOW TO DO A DRAWING OF THEM. LET THEM KNOW THAT YOU CARE ABOUT THEM, TOO.

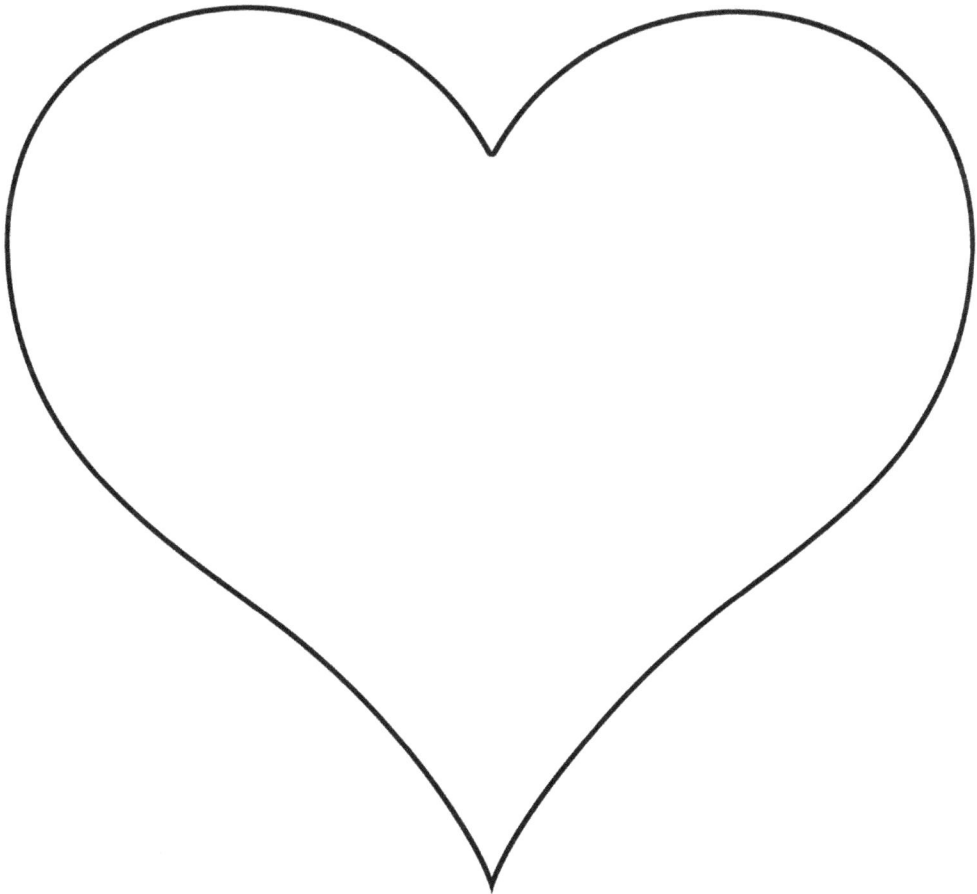

ALSO, REMEMBER THAT BULLIES ARE PEOPLE, TOO

SOMETIMES, THOSE WHO BULLY US ARE ALSO VICTIMS OF PAIN AND HURT, AND EVEN HATE. THEY MAY NEED A FRIEND BUT NOT KNOW HOW TO SAY IT.

IT'S HARD TO BE NICE TO SOMEONE BEING MEAN TO YOU, BUT IT'S ALSO HARD TO BE MEAN TO SOMEONE WHO'S BEING NICE.

YOUR PERSONAL
BADGE OF COURAGE

IT TAKES A LOT OF BRAVERY TO STAND
UP TO SOMEONE WHO IS BULLYING YOU.
COLOR IN YOUR BADGE OF COURAGE.

WE CAN ALL BE HEROES

WE ALL HAVE THE POWER TO CHANGE A
PERSON'S LIFE BY DOING THE RIGHT THING.
WE CAN ALL BE HEROES.

YOU DON'T NEED SUPER POWERS

WHO ARE SOME HEROES YOU KNOW?
HEROES OFTEN AREN'T FAMOUS. ALL THAT
MATTERS IS THAT THEY HAVE HEROIC QUALITIES.

YOU CAN BE A HERO, TOO

WHAT ARE SOME OF THE WAYS THAT YOU CAN BE A HERO FOR OTHERS?

LET'S STOP BULLYING TODAY

BULLYING HAS A NEGATIVE IMPACT ON EVERYONE IN SOCIETY—AND SHOULD NEVER BE ACCEPTABLE. TOGETHER, WE CAN EACH MAKE A DIFFERENCE AND IMPROVE OUR COMMUNITY.

KRISTIN WESTBERG

BIOGRAPHY

With nine years of middle school teaching experience as well as an M.S. in Youth Development Leadership and a M.Ed. in Higher Ed Administration, **Kristin Westberg** thoroughly understands the practice and theory of creating an environment that is intolerant of bullying. As part of her role as RTC's director of operations, Kristin designs curriculum and creates workbooks and other teaching tools. Her work with *Heroes in the Classroom* is a culmination of her varied expertise.

As her own children progress through school, Kristin tries to instill the lessons in this workbook in them, in hopes that they will be "upstanders"—unwilling to ignore, encourage, or tolerate bullying.

JEFFREY D. KRUKAR, PH.D.

BIOGRAPHY

Jeffrey D. Krukar, Ph.D. is a licensed psychologist and certified school psychologist with more than 20 years of experience working with children and families in a variety of settings, including community based group homes, vocational rehabilitation services, residential treatment, juvenile corrections, public schools, and private practice. He earned his Ph.D. in educational psychology, with a school psychology specialization and psychology minor, from the University of Wisconsin-Milwaukee. Dr. Krukar is a registrant of the National Register of Health Service Providers in Psychology, and is also a member of the American Psychological Association.

As the psychologist at Genesee Lake School in Oconomowoc, WI, Dr. Krukar believes it truly takes a village to raise a child—to strengthen developmental foundations in relating, communicating, and thinking—so they can successfully return to their families and communities. Dr. Krukar hopes the ORP Library of disabilities books will bring to light the stories of children and families to a world that is generally not aware of their challenges and successes, as well as offer a sense of hope to those currently on this journey. His deepest hope is that some of the concepts in these books resonate with parents and professionals working with kids with disabilities, and offer possibilities that will help kids achieve their maximum potential and life enjoyment.

PAMELA DeLOATCH

BIOGRAPHY

Pamela DeLoatch is a writer, editor, and storyteller. With a journalism degree from American University and an MBA from Duke University's Fuqua School of Business, Pamela crafts writing to educate, entertain, and engage. Over a period of eight months, Pamela immersed herself in the story of a boy named Jason to create the first book about bullying in the ORP Library, *Classroom Heroes*, and how those who cared about him challenged the pervasiveness of bullying by changing their concept of individual accountability.

While neither *Classroom Heroes* nor *Heroes in the Classroom* may present the miracle cure to end all bullying, Pamela hopes that those who read them will come away with an understanding of how deeply bullying affects everyone, along with the realization that each of us can make a difference, even one person at a time.

JAMES G. BALESTRIERI

BIOGRAPHY

James G. Balestrieri is currently the CEO of Oconomowoc Residential Programs, Inc. (ORP). He has worked in the human services field for 40 years, holding positions that run the gamut to include assistant maintenance, assistant cook, direct care worker, teacher's aide, summer camp counselor, bookkeeper, business administrator, marketing director, CFO, and CEO. Jim graduated from Marquette University with a B.S. in Business Administration (1977) and a Master's in Business Administration with an emphasis in Marketing (1988). He is also a Certified Public Accountant (Wisconsin—1982). Jim has a passion for creatively addressing the needs of those with impairments by managing the inherent stress among funding, programming, and profitability. He believes that those with a disability enjoy rights and protections that were created by the hard-fought efforts of those who came before them; that the Civil Rights movement is not just for minority groups; and that people with disabilities have a right to find their place in the world and to achieve their maximum potential as individuals. For more information, see *www.orp.com*.

ABOUT ORP

Oconomowoc Residential Programs, Inc. is an employee-owned family of companies whose mission is to make a difference in the lives of people with disabilities. Our dedicated staff of 2,000 employee owners provides quality services and professional care to more than 1,700 children, adolescents, and adults with special needs. ORP provides a continuum of care, including residential therapeutic education, community-based residential services, support services, respite care, treatment programs, and day services. The individuals in our care include people with developmental disabilities, physical disabilities, and intellectual disabilities. **Our guiding principle is passion:** a passion for the people we serve and for the work we do. For a comprehensive look at our programs and people, please visit *www.orp.com*.

ORP offers residential therapeutic education programs and alternative day schools among its array of services. These programs offer developmentally appropriate education and treatment for children, adolescents, and young adults in settings specially attuned to their needs. We provide special programs for students with specific academic and social issues relative to a wide range of disabilities, including autistic disorder, Asperger's disorder, mental retardation, anxiety disorders, depression, bipolar disorder, reactive attachment disorder, attention deficit disorder, Prader-Willi Syndrome, and other disabilities.

Genesee Lake School is a nationally recognized provider of comprehensive residential treatment, educational, and vocational services for children, adolescents, and young adults with emotional, mental health, neurological, or developmental disabilities. GLS has specific expertise in Autism Spectrum Disorders, anxiety and mood disorders, and behavioral disorders. We provide an individualized, person-centered, integrated team approach, which emphasizes positive behavioral support, therapeutic relationships, and developmentally appropriate practices. Our goal is to assist each individual to acquire skills to live, learn, and succeed in a community-based, less restrictive environment. GLS is particularly known for its high quality educational services for residential and day school students.

Genesee Lake School / Admissions Director
36100 Genesee Lake Road
Oconomowoc, WI 53066
262-569-5510
http://www.geneseelakeschool.com

T.C. Harris School is located in an attractive setting in Lafayette, Indiana. T.C. Harris teaches skills to last a lifetime, through a full therapeutic program as well as day school and other services.

T.C. Harris School / Admissions Director
3700 Rome Drive
Lafayette, IN 47905
765-448-4220
http://www.tcharris.com

T.C. Harris Academy is a private school option, in the local community, that works not only to stabilize a student's behavior in a therapeutic setting, but also help them thrive academically. Our goal is simple: provide students with the skills they need to function effectively and achieve greater success.

T.C. Harris Academy
3746 Rome Drive
Lafayette, IN 47905
765-448-9989
http://www.tcharris.com

Transitions Academy provides behavioral health and educational services to adolescents in a 24-hour structured residential setting. Treatment services are offered that are best practice and evidence based, targeting social, emotional, behavioral, and mental health impairments. Transitions Academy serves children from throughout the United States.

Transitions Academy / Admissions Director
11075 North Pennsylvania Street
Indianapolis, IN 46280
Toll Free: 1-844-488-0448
admissions@transitions-academy.com

The Richardson School is a day school in West Allis, Wisconsin that provides an effective, positive alternative education environment serving children from Milwaukee, Beloit, and their surrounding communities.

The Richardson School / Director
6753 West Roger Street
West Allis, WI 53219
414-540-8500
http://www.richardsonschool.com

BULLYING

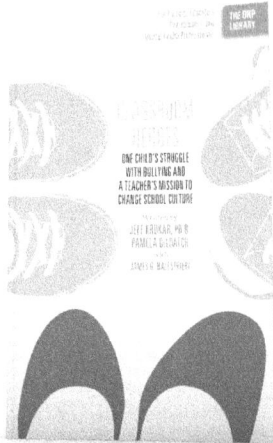

CLASSROOM HEROES
ONE CHILD'S STRUGGLE WITH
BULLYING AND A TEACHER'S MISSION
TO CHANGE SCHOOL CULTURE

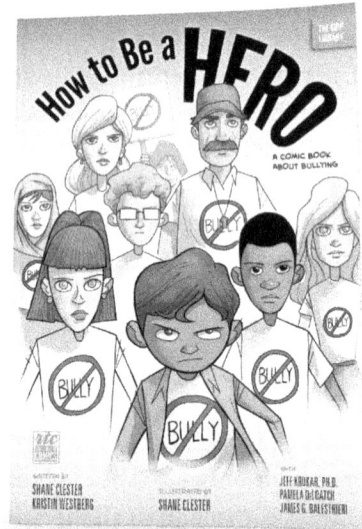

HOW TO BE A HERO
A COMIC BOOK
ABOUT BULLYING

Nearly one third of all school children face physical, verbal, social, or cyber bullying on a regular basis. Educators and parents search for ways to end bullying, but as that behavior becomes more sophisticated, it's harder to recognize and stop. In *Classroom Heroes*, Jason is a quiet, socially awkward seventh grader who has long suffered bullying in silence. His parents notice him becoming angrier and more withdrawn, but they don't realize the scope of the problem until one bully takes it too far—and one teacher acts on her determination to stop it. Both *Classroom Heroes* and *How to Be a Hero*—along with a supporting coloring book (*Heroes in the Classroom*) and curriculum guide (*Those Who Bully and Those Who Are Bullied*)—recognize that stopping bullying requires a change in mindset: adults and children must create a community that simply does not tolerate bullying. These books provide practical yet very effective strategies to end bullying, one student at a time.

ASPERGER'S DISORDER

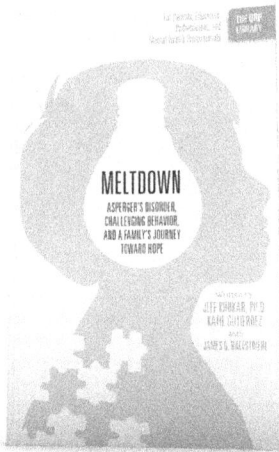

MELTDOWN
ASPERGER'S DISORDER, CHALLENGING BEHAVIOR, AND A FAMILY'S JOURNEY TOWARD HOPE

MELTING DOWN
A COMIC FOR KIDS WITH ASPERGER'S DISORDER AND CHALLENGING BEHAVIOR

Meltdown and its companion comic book, *Melting Down*, are both based on the fictional story of Benjamin, a boy diagnosed with Asperger's disorder and additional challenging behavior. From the time Benjamin is a toddler, he and his parents know he is different: he doesn't play with his sister, refuses to make eye contact, and doesn't communicate well with others. And his tantrums are not like normal tantrums; they're meltdowns that will eventually make regular schooling—and day-to-day life—impossible. Both the prose book, intended for parents, educators, and mental health professionals, and the comic for the kids themselves demonstrate that the journey toward hope isn't simple . . . but with the right tools and teammates, it's possible.

AUTISM SPECTRUM DISORDER

MR. INCREDIBLE

A STORY ABOUT AUTISM, OVERCOMING
CHALLENGING BEHAVIOR, AND A FAMILY'S
FIGHT FOR SPECIAL EDUCATION RIGHTS

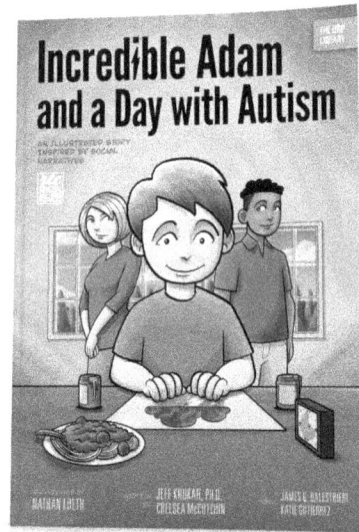

INCREDIBLE ADAM
AND A DAY WITH AUTISM

AN ILLUSTRATED STORY
INSPIRED BY SOCIAL NARRATIVES

Mr. Incredible shares the fictional story of Adam, a boy diagnosed with autistic disorder. On Adam's first birthday, his mother recognizes that something is different about him: he recoils from the touch of his family, preferring to accept physical contact only in the cool water of the family's pool. As Adam grows older, he avoids eye contact, is largely nonverbal, and has very specific ways of getting through the day; when those habits are disrupted, intense meltdowns and self-harmful behavior follow. From seeking a diagnosis to advocating for special education services, from keeping Adam safe to discovering his strengths, his family becomes his biggest champion. The journey to realizing Adam's potential isn't easy, but with hope, love, and the right tools and teammates, they find that Adam truly is *Mr. Incredible*. The companion comic in this series, inspired by social stories, offers an innovative, dynamic way to guide children—and parents, educators, and caregivers—through some of the daily struggles experienced by those with autism.

FAMILY SUPPORT

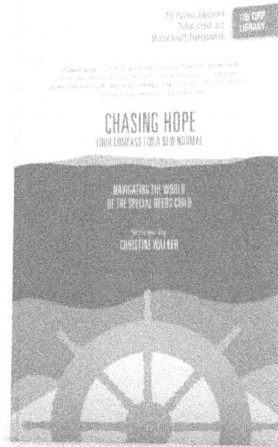

CHASING HOPE
YOUR COMPASS FOR A NEW NORMAL
NAVIGATING THE WORLD OF THE SPECIAL NEEDS CHILD

Schuyler Walker was just four years old when he was diagnosed with autism, bipolar disorder, and ADHD. In 2004, childhood mental illness was rarely talked about or understood. With knowledge and resources scarce, Schuyler's mom, Christine, navigated a lonely maze to determine what treatments, medications, and therapies could benefit her son. In the ten years since his diagnosis, Christine has often wished she had a "how to" guide that would provide the real mom-to-mom information she needed to survive the day and, in the end, help her family navigate the maze with knowledge, humor, grace, and love. Christine may not have had a manual at the beginning of her journey, but she hopes this book will serve as yours.

PRADER-WILLI SYNDROME

INSATIABLE

A PRADER-WILL STORY

ULTRA-VIOLET

ONE GIRL'S
PRADER-WILLI STORY

Estimated to occur once in every 15,000 births, Prader-Willi Syndrome is a rare genetic disorder that includes features of cognitive disabilities, problem behaviors, and, most pervasively, chronic hunger that leads to dangerous overeating and its life-threatening consequences. *Insatiable: A Prader-Willi Story* and its companion comic book, *Ultra-Violet: One Girl's Prader-Willi Story*, draw on dozens of intensive interviews to offer insight into the world of those struggling with Prader-Willi Syndrome. Both books tell the fictional story of Violet, a vivacious young girl born with the disorder, and her family, who—with the help of experts—will not give up their quest to give her a healthy and happy life.

REACTIVE ATTACHMENT DISORDER

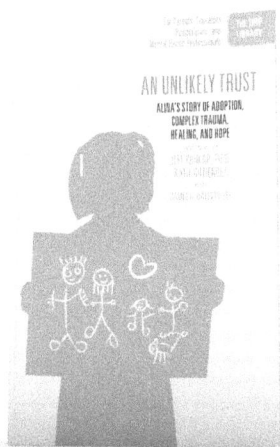

AN UNLIKELY TRUST
ALINA'S STORY OF ADOPTION, COMPLEX TRAUMA, HEALING, AND HOPE

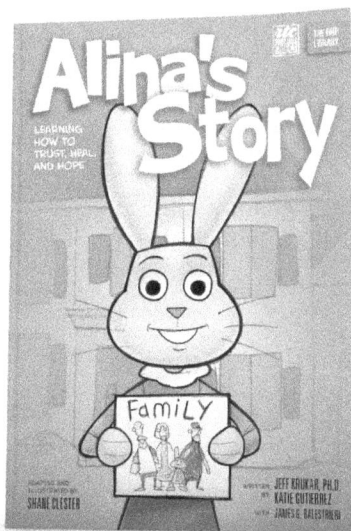

ALINA'S STORY
LEARNING HOW TO TRUST, HEAL, AND HOPE

An Unlikely Trust: Alina's Story of Adoption, Complex Trauma, Healing, and Hope, and its companion children's book, *Alina's Story*, share the journey of Alina, a young girl adopted from Russia. After living in an orphanage during her early life, Alina is unequipped to cope with the complexities of the outside world. She has a deep mistrust of others and finds it difficult to talk about her feelings. When she is frightened, overwhelmed, or confused, she lashes out in rages that scare her family. Alina's parents know she needs help and work endlessly to find it for her, eventually discovering a special school that will teach Alina new skills. Slowly, Alina gets better at expressing her feelings and solving problems. For the first time in her life, she realizes she is truly safe and loved . . . and capable of loving in return.

Also look for books on children and psychotropic medications coming soon!

www.ingramcontent.com/pod-product-compliance
Lightning Source LLC
Chambersburg PA
CBHW081230020426
42331CB00012B/3116